Copyright © 2018

Book Beetle Publishing

Melbourne, Australia

ISBN: 978-0-9954141-2-9

Written by Matthey Hartley

Illustrated by Lori Escobar

All rights reserved. No part of this publication may be reproduced in any form by any electronic or mechanical means including photocopying, recording, or information storage and retrieval without permission in writing from the author.

All events and characters portrayed are purely fictional and any likeness to any persons living or dead is purely coincidental.

Contents

The Super Speech	6
My Forgetful Teacher	8
My Smelly Locker	10
What I Learnt At School	12
The Protest	14
The Shopping List	16
Parent Teacher Night	18
Walking to School	20
The Magician	22
The Excursion	24
My Family	26
The Sneeze	28
The Silent Smell	30
The School Band	32
My Parents Are In Hiding	34
The Game Boy	36
The Teachers Are In Trouble	38
The Swimming Sports	40
Busting	42
Lunch	44
Show and Tell	46

Matthew Hartley was born in Melbourne, Australia. From an early age he loved to draw and write, and dreamed of becoming an author when he grew up.

He wrote his first book in primary school, which was called Psycho Robots. He printed some copies and the book was a huge hit with his classmates, but it did not receive wider recognition.

Over the years he has published several books and wrote a script for a short cartoon that was shown at ACMI. He's also been published in various magazines such as Gameinformer.

In 2016 he published the humorous poetry collection, A Fright in the Night and Other Rhymes.

He is currently working on another poetry book and his first book series.

In his spare time Matthew likes reading and gaming.

To learn more about Matthew's work, check out his Facebook group @authormatthewhartley. You can also contact him by writing to authormhartley@gmail.com

Lori Escobar is a digital and fine artist who refined her skills at the Maryland Institute College of Art in Baltimore, USA. She holds a BFA in illustration and a concentration in ceramics.

While Lori has multiple ongoing freelance projects in logo design and traditional painting (to name a few!), she works as an illustrator at Fifth Sun in Chico, California creating t-shirt designs and apparel.

In her spare time she paints murals and is also working on a stop-motion animation project.

You can contact Lori and see samples of her work at www.loriesque.com

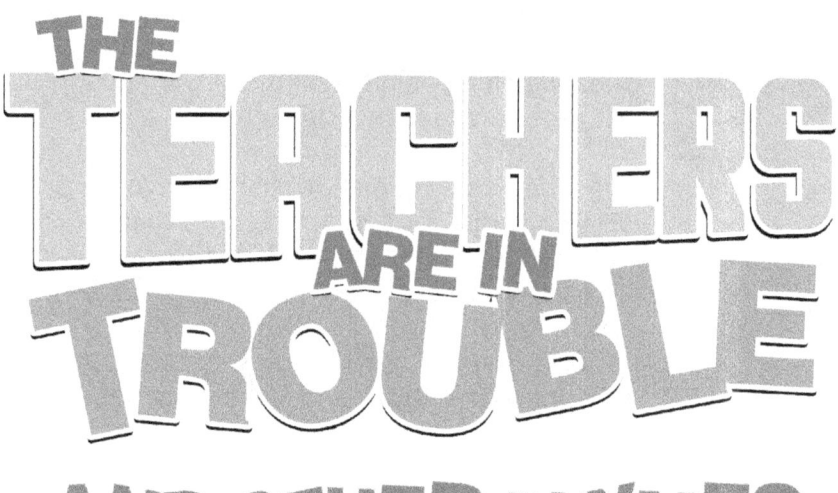

THE TEACHERS ARE IN TROUBLE
AND OTHER RHYMES

By
Matthew Hartley

Illustrated by
Lori Escobar

BOOK BEETLE PUBLISHING

Dancing Disasters	48
The Forgetful Student	50
The Learner	52
My Birthday Party	54
My Teacher Took My iPod	56
Greens	58
My Nightmares	60
My Sister's Dress	62
Dad's Cooking	64
Faking It	66
The Canteen	68
The School Play	70
Ted's Talent	72
The Kiss	74
The School Bus	76
My Paper Plane	78
The Winning Shot	80
The School Photo	82
The End of School	84

The Super Speech

When I go to assembly
I'm usually bored.
But the Principal's speech
left us floored.

He said, 'School has changed,
you can wear free dress.
And you won't get hassled
if your desk is a mess.

Those at this school
shouldn't feel troubled.
So homework's been banned
and play time's been doubled.

The canteen now has junk food,
if you want a snack.
And if the teacher scolds you,
you're free to talk right back.

You'll also never have to sit
another boring test.
All of these new changes
I think are for the best.'

But this all too perfect state of things,
very quickly passed.
Because Mr Oxley woke me up
and I was back in class.

My Forgetful Teacher

My teacher still forgets my name,
she calls me Luke and Bill.
And once, to my astonishment,
she even called me Jill!

Many times I've told her,
my actual name is Nick.
But I don't believe she listens,
'cause then she called me 'Rick.'

Her memory really bothers me,
but there's nothing I can do.
I've really tried my hardest
to stop the, 'Who are you?'

I even made a giant sign,
I thought that's all I'd need.
Then later I was shocked to learn
my teacher couldn't read!

My Smelly Locker

My locker needed tidying,
it was bursting full of junk.
It smelled really disgusting,
much worse than any skunk.

I had to hold my nose
to help avoid the smell.
I think I found an orange,
but it was difficult to tell.

All the lunches that I found
were green with furry mould.
I was really quite embarrassed,
as some were eight months old.

Cleaning out my locker,
delivered many shocks.
I found a hundred thousand ants
and some odd and smelly socks.

And then I found some homework,
forgotten school books too.
And that's when I gave up the cleaning,
I had much better things I could do.

What I Learnt At School

Today my mother asked me,
'What did you learn at school?'
I said, 'I learnt a lot of things
I think are pretty cool.'

I told her that I'd learnt a way
to stand out in a crowd.
You wait until it's silent,
and then you burp quite loud.

I also learnt to gross out girls,
by showing them a worm.
It's really quite hilarious
to watch them as they squirm.

Jimmy taught me swear words
and how to forge a note.
I also learnt some acting
and faked a dry, sore throat.

I've found some really clever ways
to cheat on all my tests.
All these things I've learnt at school
I think that they're the best.'

I thought my mother would be pleased,
but she began to fret.
She said, 'These things that you have learned,
I think you'd best forget.'

The Protest

Chant 1

We protest, we protest,
homework should be laid to rest.

Chant 2

Homework is a no-no,
so it has to go-go.

Chant 3

This is our demand,
homework should be banned.

Chant 4

Everybody sing this rhyme,
homework is a waste of time.

The Shopping List

My Mum had sent me shopping,
with a list of food to get.
I was glad to have a shopping list,
so I'd not forget.

Arriving at the corner store,
I soon found something nice.
A pack of chocolate ice creams,
on sale for half the price.

I also found potato chips
and a great big chocolate block.
The store had lots of doughnuts,
but soon were out of stock.

The popcorn looked appealing,
so I picked up twenty packs.
Then it was time to go back home,
with all my tasty snacks.

Back at home I greeted Mum,
she yelled and shook her fist.
Nothing that I'd bought that day
was on the shopping list.

Parent Teacher Night

Tonight my teacher met my Dad,
who acted like a clown.
He kept on running round until
my teacher said, 'Sit down!'

But Dad pretended he was deaf,
then jumped up on his chair.
And then he said, 'Look! Spider!'
to give us all a scare.

And then he poked his tongue out,
and hollered out, 'Surprise!'
My teacher frowned and looked at Mum,
who shrugged and rolled her eyes.

My teacher said my conduct
at school is really bad.
But now she finally understands,
I've learnt it all from Dad.

Walking to School

As I began the walk to school,
it seemed a pleasant day.
But soon things started happening
to take those thoughts away.

I felt a slippery something,
right beneath my shoe.
The awful smell alerted me
that it was doggy-do.

Then I passed Miss Fletcher's house,
whose bulldogs then attacked.
She'd left her gate wide open,
I was almost doggy snacks!

Mr Archer turned on his sprinkler,
as I was walking by.
He wasn't even sorry,
he smiled and then said, 'Hi.'

To my relief the sun was out
and I quickly started to dry.
But then some stormy clouds appeared
and drenched me from the sky.

I thought my woes were over,
once at school and through the gate.
But I promptly got detention
'cause my teacher said, 'You're late!'

The Magician

A magician came to school
and I really liked his show.
I wonder how he did his tricks,
I'd really like to know.

First he tapped his top hat
and said a magic word.
A fluffy bunny jumped out,
followed by a bird.

Then he told us, 'I can fly,'
and soon began to rise.
I couldn't see one single string,
which filled me with surprise.

But the last trick was the best,
he used a volunteer.
My teacher put her hand up
and he made her disappear.

The Excursion

Today we had an excursion
and what a catastrophe.
We really should have stayed at school,
and I think that you'll agree.

Bill and Jen were really sick;
and vomited in the aisle.
Someone else let off some gas,
which lingered for a while.

Miss Marshal did a head count,
and there was one more kid to find.
Then suddenly she realised
she'd left poor Jack behind.

Our driver was getting angry,
'cause the traffic was so slow.
Jim kept putting his hand up,
saying, 'I need to go.'

Finally we reached the zoo,
where we were greeted with rain.
As nobody brought an umbrella,
we drove to school again.

My Family

I think my family's crazy
and soon you'll know just why.
When our Mum yelled, 'Food fight!'
the food began to fly.

My brother was the first one hit,
with a giant loaf of bread.
He was lucky it was nice and soft,
as it hit him in the head.

My sister ducked for cover,
in the hope that she'd stay clean.
But then she shouted, 'I am hit!'
and, 'Dad, you're really mean.'

But soon she had her sweet revenge
and gave a hearty laugh.
Dad was drenched with gravy
and he said, 'I need a bath.'

Then our Mum came under siege,
demanding, 'I need aid.'
But no one came to help,
so she was soaked with lemonade.

I jumped up on the kitchen chair
and called them a disgrace.
But Mum just laughed
and threw a chicken pie toward my face.

At last the food fight ended
and no one had been hurt.
But I started feeling nervous
when Mum brought out dessert.

The Sneeze

When my teacher pulled the blind,
daylight stung her eyes.
Then what happened next to her,
took her by surprise.

She said, 'I think I'm going to sneeze,
I'll try and hold it in.'
We could see that she was struggling,
with a fight she couldn't win.

She tried so hard to stop herself,
what ever could she do?
My teacher couldn't hold it back,
she screamed a loud, 'Achoo!'

She should have covered up her nose,
I guess that she forgot.
I wish that she'd remembered though,
'cause now we're drenched in snot.

The Silent Smell

Everyone could smell it,
although there'd been no sound.
The culprit was in hiding,
afraid of being found.

I said that, 'Tim's responsible
for that awful, rotten smell.
He's looking quite suspicious,
the truth he ought to tell.'

He said my accusation
had tarnished up his name.
He claimed he hadn't done it
and others were to blame.

So then I questioned Jenny
and said, 'I think it's you.'
But Jenny looked bewildered
and claimed it wasn't true.

Benjamin was picked on next
which made him really mad.
'I sometimes smell,' he then confessed,
'but mine are not that bad.'

But then the class accused poor me,
a charge that I denied.
And then the smelly silence broke
and they knew that I had lied.

The School Band

Today at school our eager band
had to play a song.
Ms Nash was our conductor
and she said it sounded wrong.

Jim's guitar was cranking,
its volume turned to high.
Ms Nash had covered both her ears,
to dull the battle cry.

Gregory was playing drums,
but couldn't get the beat.
He managed to achieve this
when he played with both his feet.

Tim had found a special way
of playing his recorder.
The instrument went up his nose,
which added more disorder.

I was on the bagpipes,
but was told I couldn't play.
When drawing close to Mrs Nash,
she yelled out, 'Get away!'

And as our little band had planned,
our music gave no thrills.
Mrs Nash escaped to find,
her migraine headache pills.

My Parents Are In Hiding

My parents look worried,
they're trying to hide.
The house lights are off
and they won't go outside.

The telephone's ringing,
they won't take the call.
The answering machine says
they've gone to Nepal.

The doorbell rang this morning
and I heard the loudest knock.
My teacher stood outside the house
and Mum went into shock.

My parents thought a chat
would not be for the best.
They couldn't talk about the 'F'
they'd found on my latest test.

The Game Boy

Tonight I was Batman
and then Nathan Drake.
Metal Gear was the game
where I turned into Snake.

In Skyrim I was a wood elf
and had a high level of sneak.
Racing next as Mario,
I was on a winning streak.

Then I morphed into Lara Croft
and was on a special quest.
I searched a scary darkened tomb,
and found a treasure chest.

But now I'm feeling really bad,
because I'm only me.
I've lots of homework left to do
and it's nearly half past three!

The Teachers Are In Trouble

The teachers are in trouble,
they've got a lot to fear.
Every single one of them says,
'I hate this time of year.'

The teachers are on high alert,
they all have little doubt.
They know that we have plans for them,
we wish to carry out.

The teachers at our school
are all so easy to trick.
They'll fall for rubber spiders,
or some yucky plastic sick.

If you're a teacher you'd better watch out,
you'll not be safe at school.
The kids are trying their very best
to make you an April Fool!'

The Swimming Sports

Today we had our swimming sports,
I felt like such a fool.
I belly-flopped and caused a splash
that nearly drained the pool.

Then when Nick's turn came to dive,
he found he couldn't swim.
My teachers' clothes got soaking wet,
diving after him.

Everyone in the freestyle race,
was swimming awkward style.
It should have been a quick event,
but it lasted quite awhile.

Ben, my friend, was smiling
at everybody's troubles.
But then around his Speedos
we saw a lot of bubbles.

The teachers called the races off,
which came as no surprise.
The chlorine in the swimming pool
was stinging all our eyes.

It's such a shame, the swimming sports,
didn't go as planned.
Next time sport's day comes around,
we'll have them on dry land.

Busting

During our mathematics class
I really felt the worst.
My bladder was expanding
and I thought I'd probably burst.

I put my hand up straight and tall,
my teacher glared at me.
'What do you want?' she demanded.
'I really need to pee.'

She said, 'You always dawdle,
'cause you just don't want to learn.
Last time you left the classroom,
you took hours to return.'

'I promise that won't happen now,
it really won't I swear.'
My teacher pondered for awhile,
as I squirmed upon my chair.

She said to go, but hurry back,
which was nice, I must declare.
But now I have to tell her
that I need new underwear.

Lunch

Each time I check my lunch box,
there's nothing new in there.
I'd rather something different,
but my Mother doesn't care.

So even though I'm famished,
I take the smallest bite.
The reason that I do this is,
I'm sick of Vegemite!

I've tried to ask my friends
if they've any food to spare,
but they just shake their heads,
because they just don't want to share.

So I have to watch them munching on
their chocolates and their chips.
And they never show me pity,
as I sit and lick my lips.

When I go home, nobody there
can understand my plight.
Guess what was served for dinner?
Your guess is probably right.

Show and Tell

Today the class had show and tell,
which didn't go as planned.
When Mrs Reed recovers
I think it might be banned.

Jess brought in her parrot
and the class was quite impressed.
But Mrs Reed was pooped on,
which made her quite depressed.

Then Dan took out his little mouse,
which gave her quite a scare.
She then began to scream out loud
and jumped up on her chair.

Then she saw my python
and let out a piercing shout.
She said, 'He looks revolting!'
and then she passed right out.

Dancing Disasters

It was the night of the school Spring dance
and the hall was completely packed.
But the girls and boys just sat and stared,
they were too afraid to act.

Finally Jeff walked up to Kate,
hoping for a dance.
But Kate turned up her little nose
replying, 'Not a chance.'

William started dancing round,
but had to call it quits.
He ripped his pants right open,
trying to do the splits.

David was twirling his partner,
too many times around.
The poor girl said, 'I'm dizzy,'
and tumbled to the ground.

Tim asked Jessica onto the floor
she replied with, 'I suppose.'
She very quickly soon stormed off,
when he stepped on all her toes.

Then the DJ put on a song,
aiming to pack the floor.
But everybody ran instead
toward the exit door.

The Forgetful Student

When I arrived at school today
I felt extremely bad.
I'd forgotten to do my homework
and my teacher got quite mad.

She said, 'You're very forgetful,'
and she tapped me on the head.
'Do you think you can fix the problem?'
'Of course I can,' I said.

When I awoke next morning,
my homework was complete.
I put it in my schoolbag,
then headed down the street.

And when I arrived at school,
I didn't know what to say.
Not a soul turned up for class,
because it was Saturday.

The Learner

My sister tried to ride her bike
and swayed from side to side.
'I don't need any help,' she said,
but she was in for a bumpy ride.

First she ran over the roses,
which had only just started to grow.
Then she made my Daddy cry,
by riding on his toe.

Next she headed toward our Mum,
who had to take a dive.
She landed on the compost and,
was lucky to be alive.

The bike veered over to Molly
and I yelled, 'Look out for the cat!'
My sister tried her best to swerve,
but now poor Molly's flat.

The bike then took another turn,
heading straight towards me.
But then my sister swiftly stopped,
colliding with a tree.

When she finally came to her senses,
she was sorry for what she'd done.
Then off she went to ride again,
'cause it was so much fun!

My Birthday Party

Today I had my birthday,
and no one was invited.
You might suppose that's really sad,
but I was quite delighted.

All my friends looked quite surprised
when told to not attend.
I had to reassure them all
that I was still their friend.

Though none of them were happy,
I really didn't care.
The cake was just delicious,
so I'm glad I didn't share.

My Teacher Took My iPod

My teacher took my iPod
and I'll never get it back.
Deciding that she'd try it out,
she found a groovy track.

First her head began to nod
and join the music's beat.
And then she started swaying
and tapping both her feet.

After that my teacher sang,
she sounded really bad.
Soon the principal arrived,
he looked extremely mad.

He ordered that she stop the noise,
but she didn't pay attention.
Still dancing she was dragged away
and now she's in detention.

Greens

Tonight the greens upon my plate
didn't stay for long.
And that's what made my Mother say,
'I think that something's wrong.'

When Mother lifted up my plate,
the greens could not be found.
I told her that I'd eaten them,
but still she looked around.

She looked beneath the table
and spied the broccoli there.
'It accidentally fell,' I said,
but Mother didn't care.

She looked inside my pockets
and peas fell on the floor.
I said that she had found them all,
but Mother knew the score.

And so she kept on searching,
she rearranged my shirt.
All the other peas rolled out,
no ice cream for dessert.

My Nightmares

My parents woke me up last night,
because they heard my screams.
They asked me what the problem was,
I told them, 'Bad dreams.'

Some aliens had kidnapped me
and wished to do a test.
But what they did was horrible,
I won't describe the rest.

Then I sailed on a pirate ship
and the captain really stank.
But when I refused to wash the deck,
he made me walk the plank.

Next I met a dragon,
who made an awful boast.
Every person that he'd met
now looked like well-done toast.

I managed to escape his cave,
but crashed into a ghoul.
But the scariest part of the nightmare
was ending up at school.

My Sister's Dress

I've got another hand me down
and I'm not at all impressed.
My sister's got some brand new clothes,
but look at how *I'm* dressed!

Mum thinks I look pretty,
but I'm feeling like a fool.
Not one boy I know of
has to wear a dress to school.

Dad's Cooking

It is long past my dinner time
and I'm feeling blue.
Dad believes that he's a chef,
but he doesn't have a clue.

The leg of lamb is ruined
and so is the tuna-bake.
He doesn't heed the cooking times,
a really big mistake!

But Dad refused to pull the plug,
and so he tackled toast.
But even this was difficult,
he burnt it like the roast.

Now my stomach's grumbling,
this happens every day.
Dad repeats his usual words,
'Let's order take-away.'

Faking It

Today I really wanted to sleep,
as school just makes me blue.
And so I decided to stay at home,
telling Mum I had the flu.

Instead she pulled my bed sheets off,
she wasn't that easy to fool.
'You don't have the flu,' she said,
'Get your butt to school.'

And so I bounded out of bed
and very soon was dressed.
I knew I'd soon be back at school
feeling pretty stressed.

I wish I didn't feel so scared.
I wish I felt invincible.
But I absolutely cannot handle
being the school principal.

The Canteen

Today I went to the canteen,
to eat and quench my thirst.
The line was really long,
I wished I'd got there first.

My stomach started grumbling,
as I waited for my food.
Then a boy pushed in front,
which was really very rude.

I noticed on my wrist-watch,
the minutes tick away.
If the line did not move faster
I'd miss out on my play.

When I'm feeling hungry
I end up getting mad.
And so I started screaming,
'The service here is bad!'

After a really painful wait,
I finally reached the front.
The lunch lady liked a chat,
but I was very blunt.

I told the lady I would like
a pie and soda pop.
But too late; the bell rang
and so she closed up shop.

The School Play

When we performed our school play,
it didn't follow the script.
Tim tore a backdrop in half,
when he accidently tripped.

Then Ben broke out of character
and threw away his wig.
He wasn't supposed to move much,
but started doing a jig.

Then Angelique came out to sing
and instead she chased a fly.
Rob pretended to murder Luke,
but Luke refused to die.

Dave couldn't see through his mask
and so he fell off stage.
Leigh hadn't learnt any of his lines
and read them off a page!

Our drama teacher loudly yelled,
'You've ruined my reputation.'
But when we all came back on stage
we witnessed a standing ovation.

Ted's Talent

My best friend loves to burp,
you should hear the awesome sound.
Because when Ted lets out a burp,
it is heard for miles around.

If you believe you can out burp Ted,
you've made a big mistake.
One day he burped so loudly
he caused the earth to quake.

I think that Ted's got talent,
of this I have no doubt.
One day when Ted let out a burp,
he knocked our teacher out.

People with a gift like Ted's,
they're often labelled twerps.
I think he should instead be praised,
and dubbed King of the burps!

The Kiss

Lucy gave me a kiss today,
which was no big deal.
She seemed to enjoy it
and asked, 'How you feel?'

I said, 'You've eaten Weet-Bix,
some whole-wheat toast and jam.
For lunch, you've had a salad roll,
with pickles, cheese and ham.'

Lucy looked embarrassed;
'However could you tell?'
So I offered her a fresh mint,
to take away the smell.

The School Bus

Today our school bus driver
was looking very mad.
Everyone was jumping around
and being really bad.

Ben set off a stink bomb,
which caused us some distress.
People tried to leave although,
the bus was an express.

Then right outside my window,
we spotted my buddy Mike.
Timmy threw an apple,
which knocked him off his bike.

Jim was trying hard to stand,
as he didn't have a seat.
When the bus suddenly stopped,
he was knocked right off his feet.

Everyone then yelled, 'Stacks on!'
and Jim was nearly squashed.
We were having such a funny time,
but that was quickly quashed.

The driver was so angry,
he couldn't keep his cool.
He made us all get off the bus,
and we had to walk to school.

My Paper Plane

Today I launched a paper plane,
it was on its maiden flight.
I watched it gliding through the air
to reach the greatest height.

Nothing could go wrong, I thought,
as we watched the plane in awe.
Of course I was mistaken,
the plane contained a flaw.

Suddenly the plane changed course,
and I was struck with fear.
It headed towards my teacher
and hit her in the rear.

The Winning Shot

With only seconds left to go,
we had to score a three.
The other team were just ahead,
so the win was left to me.

I bounced the ball around the court
and found the perfect spot.
No one else was in my way
and so I took the shot.

The ball spun all around the net
and then it tumbled in.
The other team began to cheer,
because I'd helped them win.

The School Photo

Jenny's hair's a total mess
and Tim's pulled out his shirt.
Ralph and Dan have had a fight,
so both are smeared with dirt.

Melissa's on the absent list,
because she has the flu.
And Greg's obscuring Evie,
so she's pretty absent too.

Ben looks like he's chopped in half,
and Jack's the one to blame.
Jack gave Ben a mighty shove,
that pushed him out of frame.

Dave is looking awkward,
I think he had to pee.
Leigh's not looking at the lens,
he's staring straight at Bree!

Kathy's looking tired
and both my eyes are shut.
And even poor old Mr Green
is looking like a nut.

The cameraman got one thing right,
the snap is sharp and clear.
But I hope our formal photograph
improves a lot next year.

The End of School

School had finally finished
and the teachers all went nuts.
Frankly I was quite surprised
they even had the guts.

They jumped on top of tables
and opened up champagne.
Some were even shouting,
'I'll never see you again!'

Some threw books from the windows,
a teacher swung on a fan.
None of us could quite believe,
they'd broken every ban.

We didn't know quite what to do,
and so we sat and stared.
Then they set off fireworks,
they'd really come prepared!

The teachers massive party
was absolutely great.
The final lesson of the year
was how to celebrate.

Also available from Matthew Hartley

www.ingramcontent.com/pod-product-compliance
Lightning Source LLC
Chambersburg PA
CBHW080414300426
44113CB00015B/2513